Unbelievable Pictures and Facts About New Zealand

By: Olivia Greenwood

Introduction

New Zealand is one of the safest and most beautiful countries in the entire world. It offers a very high standard of living. Today we will be learning lots of interesting things about stunning New Zealand.

Are the schools in New Zealand good?

The schools in New Zealand have gained a reputation for being some of the best in the world. The country offers a really high standard of education. The schools are generally excellent.

Are there many outdoor activities to do in New Zealand?

There is everything from hiking, surfing, skydiving, paragliding, and even bungee jumping.

Is the country a popular tourist destination?

New Zealand is an extremely popular tourist destination. It is a very well operated country, everything is safe, there is a great mix of things to do and see. People love coming to New Zealand.

What are the official languages spoken in New Zealand?

In New Zealand, they speak a few different languages. The official languages are Māori, New Zealand Sign Language, and English.

What are the local people in New Zealand called?

The local people in New Zealand are called Kiwis, this is their nickname.

Is New Zealand a popular place for people to retire?

New Zealand is an extremely popular country for people to retire. People from all ends of the world come to retire in New Zealand. The country has a very high standard of living and this makes it a great retirement destination.

Are there more people or sheep in New Zealand?

Believe it or not, there are actually more sheep in New Zealand than there are people.

Do people in New Zealand enjoy sport?

People in New Zealand love sport, their favorite sport is rugby. They are very famous all over the world for their rugby team the All Blacks.

Will you find any snakes in New Zealand?

The good news is that you will not find any snakes or poisonous animals in the entire country.

Which is the biggest city in the whole of New Zealand?

The biggest city in New Zealand is called Auckland. Many people from all over the world choose to live in Auckland.

Are there any movies that have been filmed in New Zealand?

Over the years many popular movies have been filmed in New Zealand. Some of the most popular movies include Lord of the Rings, Wolverine and The Hobbit.

Is New Zealand a child-friendly country?

New Zealand is an exceptionally child-friendly country. The entire country is fully equipped and catered for children.

Which religion do most people in New Zealand follow?

The majority of people in New Zealand follow the religion of Christianity.

What type of currency do they use in New Zealand?

The currency which they use in New Zealand is called the New Zealand Dollar.

Which city is the capital one in the country?

Have you ever heard of Wellington? This is actually the name of the capital city. Does your country have a capital city?

What type of weather can you expect in New Zealand?

New Zealand has a mixed climate depending on what part of the country you are in. During winter times it does snow in certain parts. It can become very cold and it starts to rain heavily. During the summertime, the sun is shining and the days are very warm and long.

What side of the road do people drive on in New Zealand?

In New Zealand people are required by law to drive on the left side of the road.

Exactly where can one find New Zealand?

Do you know where Australia is on the map? New Zealand is on the Southern Coast side. It may be useful to know that New Zealand is not bordered by any other country at all.

What type of landscape does New Zealand have?

New Zealand is known for its beautiful landscape. It is surrounded by mountains, valleys, hills, forests, islands, and water.

Is it safe in the country of New Zealand?

New Zealand is one of the safest countries to be in. It is very safe for both residents and tourists. You will not need to worry about your safety in New Zealand.

Printed in Great Britain
by Amazon

16295001R00025